Great Leaders of the World

Happy House

About Wise & Wide

- A systematic 6-level English reading program based on Lexile® measures
- Diverse and interesting topics chosen from the elementary curriculums of Korea and English speaking western countries
- Well-written books in various forms including fiction stories, descriptive texts, and classics retold
- The informative but original fiction stories grab your interest, leading to the easy and clear understanding of the educational content.
- Improve thinking skills with solid after-reading activities at all levels of the series.

Wise & Wide is a 6-level English reading program that consists of 60 books and each level is systematically divided by Lexile® measures. The Lexile® Framework for Reading is the most popular reading measuring system in American formal education curriculums and many English programs. Over 20 out of 50 states in the U.S. mark Lexile® measures directly on students' final report cards and over 300 well-known publishers adopt and use Lexile® measures.

Experience many kinds of readings written by professional writers from the U.S. and England. They used interesting topics that were carefully chosen after analyzing elementary curriculums from around the world including Korea, the U.S., England, and Australia among many others. Comprehensive after-reading activities including graphic organizers, speaking tasks, and After-reading Tests are ready for you.

Levels in the series and their corresponding Lexile® measures

Level	Lexile® measures	U.S. Grade
Level 1	Below 200L	Pre K - K
Level 2	190L - 400L	Lower Grade 1
Level 3	350L - 530L	Upper Grade 1
Level 4	420L - 650L	Grade 2
Level 5	520L - 940L	Grade 3 - 4
Level 6	830L - 1070L	Grade 5 - 6

＊ Smart Readers: Wise & Wide level 1 is applicable to the preschool level in the U.S.
＊ The source of the relationship between Lexile® measures and U.S. school grades: CCSS(Common Core State Standards) FOR ENGLISH LANGUAGE ARTS, APPENDIX A (2012, which is used by 45 states in the U.S.)

Topic List

	Level 1	Level 2	Level 3	Level 4	Level 5	Level 6
Book 1	Science>Biology: The hibernation of animals Story	Science>Biology: Living and nonliving things Story	Science>Biology>Animals & the Environment: Sea otters Story	Environment>Living with nature: The diver & the persimmon tree Story	Science>Biology>Animal: Amazing animals of the Amazon Story	Science>Biology: Germs, transmitted diseases Story
Book 2	Literature>World classics: Aesop's fables Story	Literature>Traditional fairy tale: Old tales about stones Story	Social Studies>Economy: To run a business to make and save money Story	Science>Biology>Plants: Photosynthesis Story	Science>Earth science: Earth's layers, earthquakes, volcanoes, and earth's atmosphere Report	Mathematics>Sequence: The golden ratio & the Fibonacci sequence Story
Book 3	Science>Physics: How shadows are formed Story	Literature>World classics: Peter Pan Story	Science>Scientific technology: Nanobots Story	Literature>Myths: World's creation stories Story	Literature>Legend: The story of King Arthur Story	Literature>Myths: Constellation myths Story
Book 4	Literature>Traditional literature: The Talmud Story	Science>Biology>Animal: Polar bears Story	Science>Biology>Animal: Mountain gorillas Story	Social Studies>Cultural anthropology: Amazing ancient cultures of the world Story	Science>Earth science: Clouds and weather Story	Literature>Human & animals: The friendship between a girl and a horse Story
Book 5	Social Studies>Ethics: Rules in daily life Story	Science>Biology: The five senses Report	Social Studies>Cultural anthropology: Astonishing festivals Report	Art>Music: Stories from two operas Story	Social Studies>World culture & history: The Renaissance Story	Sports>Board sports: Surfing & snowboarding Story
Book 6	Social Studies>World geography & travel: Tourist attractions around the world Story	Science>Biology>Animal: Dinosaurs Story	Science>Astronomy: The solar system Story	Social Studies>People: Three great people who overcame hardships Story	Science>Scientific technology: The wonderful world of robots Report	Art>Music: Composers of the Romantic Era Report
Book 7	Science>Space science: The life of astronauts Report	Social Studies>Cultural anthropology: Mythological monsters from around the world Report	Mathematics>Elementary mathematics: Numbers, measurement, shapes and data Report	Science & Social Studies>Technology & culture: Inventions from around the world Report	Art>Works of art: Famous paintings Report	Social Studies>Human & animals: Animals in action for human Report
Book 8	Social Studies>Cultural anthropology: Various living cultures of the world Story	Art>Music: Instruments in the orchestra Story	Social Studies>Life safety: Learning and using outdoor survival skills Story	Social Studies>History: The California Gold Rush Report	Social Studies & Science>Psychology: Psychology in everyday life Story	Literature>World classics: The Merchant of Venice Story
Book 9	Social Studies>Jobs: Interviews about jobs Report	Science>Scientific technology: Developments in technology in different times Story	Social Studies>Politics>Election: Running for 3rd grade class president Story	Literature>World classics: Stories of Sherlock Holmes Story	Literature>World classics: Adrift in the Pacific Story	Social Studies>History & People: Great world leaders in history Report
Book 10	Literature>Traditional fairy tale: Eastern and Western folk tales on the same theme Story	Sports>Winter sports: Various aspects of some Winter Olympic sports Report	Literature>World classics: Short stories by O. Henry Story	Sports>Ball games: Various aspects of popular ball games Report	Social Studies>History: Famous events that changed world history Report	Art & Social Studies>Art: Stories about the creation, distribution, and preservation of paintings Report

* 10 books in each level will be published.

How to Use This Book

•Before Reading

You can easily find the topic and what kind of story you are about to read.

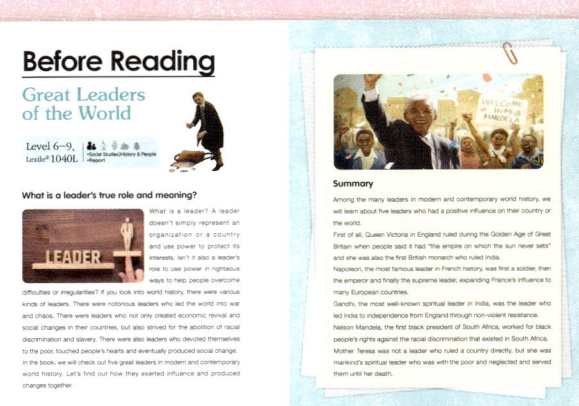

•The text

All the stories were written by professional writers from the U.S. and England, so you will read authentic and appropriate English sentences and expressions in every book in the series.

•Pop Quiz

Check out right away if you understand what you have just read by solving a pop quiz that checks your comprehension.

•Key Words

The key words and expressions on each page are listed for you to easily study them.

•Aha! Tips

Download free Korean explanations at *www.ihappyhouse.co.kr* for all of the sentences marked with "Aha!". These explain cultural, scientific, and economic knowledge or they deal with aspects of English such as grammatical structures or idiomatic expressions. There are lots of "Aha! Tips" to help you understand the text.

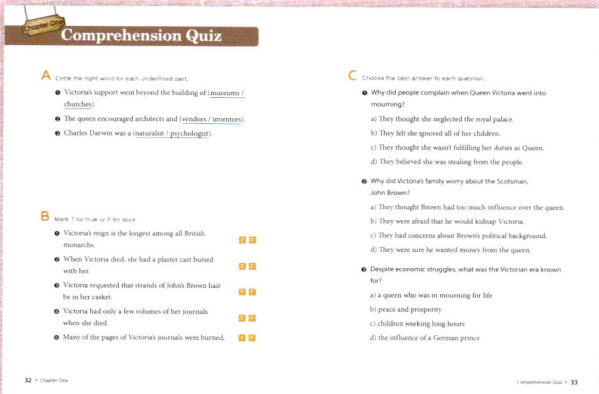

•Comprehension Quiz

After reading one chapter, solve various questions to find out if you fully understand the content.

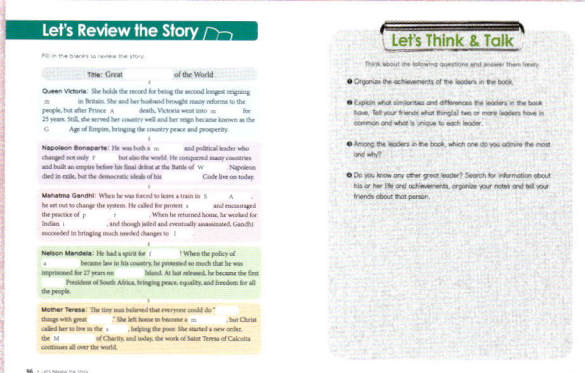

•Let's Review the Story /
•Let's Think & Talk

Fill in the blanks in the organizer to summarize the whole story. Express your own thinking and feelings about the story by answering the questions. You can build up logic and reasoning skills for your essay examinations in the future.

Appendix

Audio CD

In the CD audio book form, the texts are read vividly by American professional voice actors. (MP3 files downloaded for free)

After-reading Test

Solve an additionally provided After-reading Test for each book.

The Korean translation, Answer Keys, a Word Quiz, a Word List, and Aha! Tips for each book

You can download them for free at *www.ihappyhouse.co.kr* or *www.darakwon.co.kr*

Before Reading

Great Leaders of the World

Level 6–9, Lexile® 1040L

•Social Studies)History & People
•Report

What is a leader's true role and meaning?

What is a leader? A leader doesn't simply represent an organization or a country and use power to protect its interests. Isn't it also a leader's role to use power in righteous ways to help people overcome difficulties or irregularities? If you look into world history, there were various kinds of leaders. There were notorious leaders who led the world into war and chaos. There were leaders who not only created economic revival and social changes in their countries, but also strived for the abolition of racial discrimination and slavery. There were also leaders who devoted themselves to the poor, touched people's hearts and eventually produced social change.

In the book, we will check out five great leaders in modern and contemporary world history. Let's find out how they exerted influence and produced changes together.

Summary

Among the many leaders in modern and contemporary world history, we will learn about five leaders who had a positive influence on their country or the world.

First of all, Queen Victoria in England ruled during the Golden Age of Great Britain when people said it had "the empire on which the sun never sets" and she was also the first British monarch who ruled India.

Napoleon, the most famous leader in French history, was first a soldier, then the emperor and finally the supreme leader, expanding France's influence to many European countries.

Gandhi, the most well-known spiritual leader in India, was the leader who led India to independence from England through non-violent resistance.

Nelson Mandela, the first black president of South Africa, worked for black people's rights against the racial discrimination that existed in South Africa.

Mother Teresa was not a leader who ruled a country directly, but she was mankind's spiritual leader who was with the poor and neglected and served them until her death.

Contents

Great Leaders of the World

Great Leaders of the World

What Makes a Great Leader?

If you were asked to name the world's greatest leader from the eighteenth, nineteenth, or twentieth centuries, who would you say? Would you choose a political ruler, a king, a queen, or an emperor? Or perhaps you'd select a humanitarian, an industrial pioneer, a global inventor, or even a spiritual guide. But whomever you picked, you'd probably find that your choice for a great leader had many traits in common with those chosen by others.
Aha!

Great leaders tend to have similar characteristics. They are often ambitious and confident, and yet still have a humble and compassionate nature. They are visionaries; that is, they see the future creatively. Expect to also find courage in a great leader, though not always the kind of courage that would lead troops into battle. And don't forget persistence. These are men and women who refuse to quit, despite the odds stacked against them!

KEY WORDS

- name
- ruler
- emperor
- select
- humanitarian
- industrial
- pioneer
- spiritual
- whomever
- trait
- in common with
- tend to + *Verb*
- characteristic
- ambitious
- confident

- and yet
- humble
- compassionate
- nature
- visionary
- that is
- expect to + *Verb*
- the kind of
- troop
- persistence
- refuse
- quit
- despite
- odds
- stack against

Great leaders are trailblazers, teachers, and thinkers, and though they may have their faults, they will always leave the world a better place for future generations.

Thankfully, there have been many great recent leaders who have changed the world for the better, so it would indeed be difficult to name just one. 📖 Instead, let's take a closer look at five leaders from the last few centuries. After learning about a long-lived queen, a tenacious emperor, a surprising protester, a passionate president, and one very tiny nun, see if you can name the qualities that they all share!

KEY WORDS

- trailblazer
- thinker
- fault
- leave (leave-left-left)
- generation
- thankfully
- recent
- for the better
- indeed

- instead
- take a look (take-took-taken)
- long-lived
- tenacious
- protester
- passionate
- nun
- quality

Queen Victoria, a Royal for the Ages

In her time, Queen Victoria had the longest reign of any monarch in British history. Even today, she holds the record among all British kings and queens for being the second longest reigning monarch. But her long reign, though notable, is not what made Victoria a great leader. There was much more to this grandmother of a queen than simply all the years she wore the crown!

Almost from infancy, Victoria was destined to be queen. And so her mother, and her mother's confidant, John Conroy, raised her under strict rules. Stifled, she began to keep a diary when she was just thirteen years old. In her journals, Victoria could write and say whatever she liked, a daily habit that she continued up until ten days before she died!

KEY WORDS

- royal
- for the ages (cf. age)
- in one's time
- reign
- monarch
- hold the record (hold-held-held)
- notable
- wear the crown (wear-wore-worn)(cf. crown)
- infancy

- be destined to + Verb
- confidant
- raise
- stifle
- keep a diary (keep-kept-kept)
- journal
- habit
- up until

When, at the young age of eighteen, she took the throne, Victoria immediately asserted her own will. She sent her mother to live in rooms on the far side of the palace. And as for her mother's friend, John Conroy, she banned him from her life, never seeing him again. Instead, she relied upon her prime minister, Lord Melbourne, to advise and teach her.

The support of the British population for the crown was at an all-time low at the time of Victoria's coronation, and so the new queen had her work cut out for her. Though she made mistakes in the early days, young Victoria, with the steady help of Lord Melbourne, gradually learned what it was to be a monarch. And in doing so, she won the trust of her people.

POP QUIZ

Who helped Queen Victoria gain the support of the British people?

ⓐ her mother's confidant, John Conroy
ⓑ the prime minister, Lord Melbourne

KEY WORDS

- take the throne
- assert
- will
- on the far side of (cf. far)
- as for
- ban
- rely upon
- prime minister (cf. minister)
- Lord
- support

- population
- all-time low
- coronation
- have one's work cut out (for one) (have-had-had)
- steady
- gradually
- in doing so
- win (win-won-won)

▲ a portrait of Queen Victoria in her coronation robes
(Henry Pierce Bone [Public domain], via Wikimedia Commons)

But in 1840, Victoria married a German prince, Albert. The prime minister found that his influence was coming to an end while Albert's influence was on the rise. Though there was no doubt that Victoria had a strong mind of her own, she depended heavily on Albert. This pattern of dependence and loyalty would continue throughout her reign as Victoria developed deep and trusting

▲ Queen Victoria and Prince Albert

relationships with those who would provide invaluable aid to her. The British people, however, were not always as keen on these trusted advisors, beginning with Prince Albert. It did not change the queen's mind about him. She was completely devoted to him and wholeheartedly supported his interests, which ultimately turned out very well for Britain.

KEY WORDS

- influence
- come to an end
  (come-came-come)
- be on the rise
- there is no doubt that
  (cf. doubt)
- have a strong mind

- of one's own
- depend heavily
- dependence
- loyalty
- relationship
- provide
- invaluable

- aid
- keen on
- be devoted to
- wholeheartedly
- interest
- ultimately
- turn out

In 1851, Albert's interests in art, science, and industry led him to organize the Great Exhibition, also called the Crystal Palace Exhibition for the main building in which the event was temporarily housed.  International vendors brought their products to be displayed in this world's fair, and it was quite an impressive success. Over six million people visited the site in the six months it was in London! The profits were later used to purchase lands for both industrial and cultural museums, buildings that include some of the world's most famous museums today.

▲ the painting that describes
the Crystal Palace Exhibition in 1851
(By Read & Co. Engravers & Printers [Public domain],
via Wikimedia Commons)

KEY WORDS

- industry
- organize
- the Great Exhibition
  (*cf.* exhibition)
- Crystal Palace

- temporarily
- house
- vendor
- display
- fair

- impressive
- profit
- purchase

▲ Victoria and Albert Museum

There's the Victoria and Albert Museum, the world's largest museum of decorative arts, covering twelve and a half acres. And the Science Museum, one of England's major tourist attractions, is visited by thousands of British students every year. And any visitor to Exhibition Road in Kensington, home to these and other museums, would be sure to take a look inside the National Museum of History to see its towering dinosaur skeletons!

Victoria's support went far beyond the building of museums, though. She encouraged inventors, architects and scientists. She was a great benefactor, providing not only her influence but funds, too.  Many notable figures of her time, including the great naturalist, Charles Darwin, benefited from Victoria's support.

▲ Charles Darwin

KEY WORDS

- decorative art
- acre
- attraction
- home
- be sure to + *Verb*
- towering
- skeleton
- go beyond (go-went-gone)

- encourage
- architect
- benefactor
- not only A but (also) B
- fund
- figure
- naturalist
- benefit

Sadly, Victoria's life changed drastically around this period. Her beloved husband, Albert, died of typhoid fever in December of 1861. Albert had been a powerful influence in her life as a monarch and Victoria was devastated.

Her grief was so profound that Victoria dressed in black for the next twenty-five years! But she did not, as people believed, disappear from courtly life following her husband's death. Victoria continued her royal duties despite her mourning. She kept up correspondence and granted audiences to ministers and other public officials. Even so, people were distressed at her general absence and there were complaints that she wasn't earning her income.

KEY WORDS

- drastically
- period
- beloved
- die of
- typhoid (fever)
- devastate
- profound
- dress in black

- disappear from
- courtly
- duty
- mourning
- keep up correspondence
- grant
- audience
- public official

- even so
- distressed
- general
- absence
- complaint
- earn
- income

▲ (John Jabez Edwin Mayall [Public domain], via Wikimedia Commons)

She chose the ten-year anniversary of her husband's death to make a very public appearance. Her son, the Prince of Wales, had miraculously recovered from the same disease that had killed his father, typhoid. Victoria attended a service of Thanksgiving for him at St. Paul's Cathedral in 1871. With that appearance, she began to work her way back into the hearts of her people.

▲ Queen Victoria and John Brown
(By George Washington Wilson (1823-1893)
[Public domain], via Wikimedia Commons)

Her family, however, were not as happy with the queen. They had become increasingly concerned about a friendship between Victoria and a Scotsman and servant named John Brown. They worried about Brown's influence and her strong loyalty to him. It didn't help that sentiment in Europe was, once again, very much against the monarchy. 🌐

KEY WORDS

- anniversary
- make an appearance
  (make-made-made)
- miraculously
- recover
- disease

- attend
- service
- cathedral
- work one's way
- increasingly
- concerned about

- Scotsman
- servant
- sentiment
- be against
- monarchy

Benjamin Disraeli, her prime minister, stepped in with a new plan for the queen. In 1877, he decided that she should be named Empress of India. Although India had been a part of the crown since 1858, Victoria's new position strengthened that bond and her popularity exploded! John Brown died a few years later, and Victoria watched as Britain grew to become the most powerful nation in the world.

▲ Benjamin Disraeli
(By Cornelius Jabez Hughes, British
(1819 - 1884, London, England London, England)
[Public domain], via Wikimedia Commons)

▲ Queen Victoria
(Thomas Kennington [Public domain],
via Wikimedia Commons)

KEY WORDS

- step in
- empress
- strengthen

- bond
- popularity
- explode

- nation

Still, Victoria's nation had another side, the life that the popular author of the day, Charles Dickens, wrote about in his many novels. 🌐 Poverty was a problem during the 1800s, especially as England went from a rural economy towards the Industrial Revolution. After all, the population more than doubled in size during Victoria's reign. Many children worked as well as adults. But despite the picture painted in works such as Dickens' *A Christmas Carol*, Victoria was responsible for many reforms that eased the suffering of the poor.

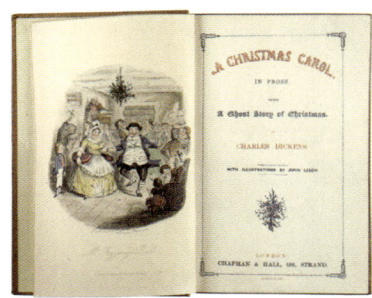

▲ *A Christmas Carol* by Charles Dickens
(John Leech [Public domain],
via Wikimedia Commons)

KEY WORDS

- of the day
- poverty
- rural economy
- Industrial Revolution

- after all
- more than
- double in size
- as well as

- be responsible for
- reform
- ease
- **suffering** (*cf.* suffer)

For example, consider the *Vaccination Act*, which made free vaccinations available. Or the *Railway Regulation Act*, which included a provision that would allow the poor to travel at a more affordable price. In 1863, in fact, the railways and the London Underground were built, thanks to her support.

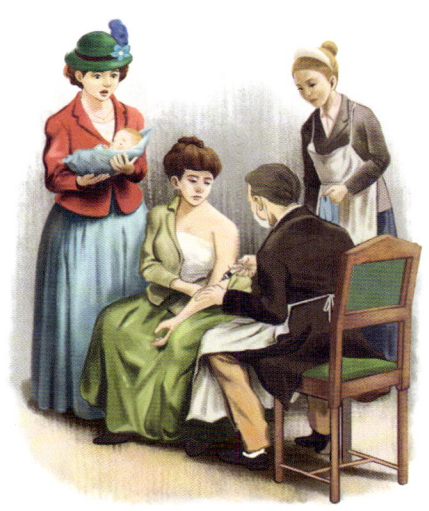

And when the monarch used chloroform during the birth of her eighth child, the use of this powerful anesthetic became widespread. No longer would women suffer through painful and natural childbirth because, after all, Queen Victoria herself had used the drug!

KEY WORDS

- vaccination
- act
- available
- regulation
- provision

- affordable
- London Underground
- thanks to
- chloroform
- anesthetic

- widespread
- no longer
- natural childbirth
- drug

There were other changes, too. Because of government reforms during her reign, England avoided much of the political upheaval going on in Europe. The monarchy doubled in size, including Canada, Australia, and parts of Africa and the South Pacific as well as India. It was said that the sun never set on the British Empire, and Victoria made sure that saying remained true for a very long time.

▲ a map that shows the expansion of the British Empire
(Walter Crane [Public domain], via Wikimedia Commons)

KEY WORDS

- government
- avoid
- upheaval
- go on

- the South Pacific
- it is said that
- set (set-set-set)
- empire

- make sure (that)
- remain

When, in January of 1901, the queen died, she had reigned for sixty-three years! Her funeral requests were both interesting and detailed. She asked for her beloved Albert's dressing gown as well as a plaster cast of his hand to be buried along with her. She also remembered her faithful servant, John Brown. A lock of his hair was buried with her. As for her journals—she had 122 volumes!—her daughter, Beatrice, was named as a literary executor, charged with carrying out her mother's wishes. She examined the queen's prolific writings and though she edited the queen's words, and even burned many of the pages, much of what Queen Victoria wrote survives today. Her words give the world an inside look into what it meant to be a monarch for most of the 1800s.

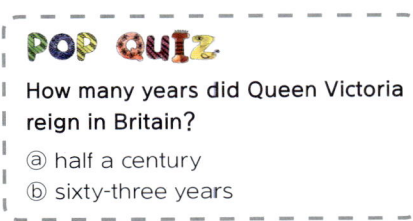

POP QUIZ

How many years did Queen Victoria reign in Britain?
ⓐ half a century
ⓑ sixty-three years

KEY WORDS

- request
- detailed
- dressing gown
- plaster cast
- bury
- along with

- faithful
- a lock of hair (*cf.* lock)
- volume
- literary executor
- be charged with
  (*cf.* charge)

- carry out
- examine
- prolific
- edit

Amazingly, Victoria's influence did not end with her death. Her nine children's marriages formed important ties throughout Europe. Her grandchildren, numbered at forty-two, guaranteed a dynasty for many years to come. And so Victoria earned the title, "Grandmother of Europe."

KEY WORDS

- tie
- throughout
- number
- guarantee
- dynasty
- for many years to come

- title
- entire
- presence
- booming
- struggle
- era

- prosperity
- remarkably
- shaky
- Golden Age of Empire
- thriving (*cf.* thrive)

It's not every day that an entire period of history is named for someone. But Victoria was a towering presence among monarchs, even though she was only five feet tall. And despite the booming population and the economic struggles, the Victorian era has become known for its peace and prosperity. The queen's remarkably long reign, though shaky at the start, is remembered as the Golden Age of Empire, with the monarchy thriving and the people thriving along with the monarch!

▼ the Victorian era refereed to as the Golden Age of Britain
(William Powell Frith [Public domain], via Wikimedia Commons)

Comprehension Quiz

A Circle the right word for each underlined part.

❶ Victoria's support went beyond the building of (<u>museums /
churches</u>).

❷ The queen encouraged architects and (<u>vendors / inventors</u>).

❸ Charles Darwin was a (<u>naturalist / psychologist</u>).

B Mark T for true or F for false.

❶ Victoria's reign is the longest among all British
monarchs. T F

❷ When Victoria died, she had a plaster cast buried
with her. T F

❸ Victoria requested that strands of John's Brown hair
be in her casket. T F

❹ Victoria had only a few volumes of her journals
when she died. T F

❺ Many of the pages of Victoria's journals were burned. T F

C Choose the best answer to each question.

❶ Why did people complain when Queen Victoria went into mourning?

a) They thought she neglected the royal palace.

b) They felt she ignored all of her children.

c) They thought she wasn't fulfilling her duties as Queen.

d) They believed she was stealing from the people.

❷ Why did Victoria's family worry about the Scotsman, John Brown?

a) They thought Brown had too much influence over the queen.

b) They were afraid that he would kidnap Victoria.

c) They had concerns about Brown's political background.

d) They were sure he wanted money from the queen.

❸ Despite economic struggles, what was the Victorian era known for?

a) a queen who was in mourning for life

b) peace and prosperity

c) children working long hours

d) the influence of a German prince

Napoleon Bonaparte, Determined Military Genius

▼ (Jacques-Louis David [Public domain], via Wikimedia Commons)

Napoleon Bonaparte was a man who did not believe in giving up. "The word impossible," he famously said, "is not in my dictionary." Time and time again, this French general and political leader appeared to be down and out, only to gloriously rise again!

Napoleon was born on the island of Corsica in 1769, just a year after the small piece of Italian land came under French rule. Not surprisingly, when he attended military school on the mainland of France, he was an outsider, knowing little of his new country's customs. No one would have guessed, looking at his rank in his graduating class—he was 47th out of 58—that this student would become one of the world's greatest military leaders!

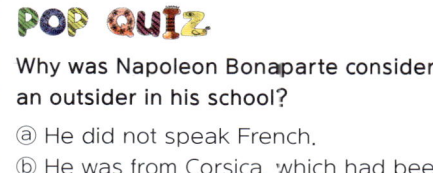

POP QUIZ

Why was Napoleon Bonaparte considered an outsider in his school?

ⓐ He did not speak French.
ⓑ He was from Corsica, which had been under Italian rule.

KEY WORDS

- determined
- believe in
- give up (give-gave-given)
- famously
- time and time again
- appear
- down and out

- gloriously
- rise again (rise-rose-risen)
- come under
- rule
- not surprisingly
- military school
- mainland

- outsider
- custom
- rank
- graduating class
- out of

In the beginning of his career, however, Napoleon's heart was with his homeland. He yearned for an independent Corsica, free of French rule. And so he returned to the island, spending his time studying strategy and waiting to make his move. 📖 It was the year 1789 and the French Revolution had already brought violent changes to the mainland's government. However, Napoleon's efforts in Corsica never got off the ground. And so the young soldier, determined to make his military mark, left his island to join forces with the new government in France. And Napoleon never looked back.

KEY WORDS

- heart
- yearn (for)
- independent
- strategy
- make one's move
- the French Revolution
- get off the ground (get-got-gotten)
- be determined to + *Verb*
- make one's mark (*cf.* mark)
- join forces with
- promote
- brigadier general

- put in charge of (put-put-put)
- ups and downs
- the Directory (= Directoire)
- republic
- face
- royalist
- insurrection
- grossly
- outnumber
- repel
- revolt
- major general

He rose rapidly in the ranks of the army. By the age of twenty-four, he had been promoted to brigadier general and put in charge of France's Army of Italy. Napoleon continued to thrive through the ups and downs of the new government. Now known as the Directory, the republic faced a royalist insurrection in 1795. Despite being grossly outnumbered, Napoleon and *his* forces repelled the revolt. He was only twenty-six years old, and was immediately promoted to major general!

▲ 13 Vendémiaire
(It was the battle between Royalist forces and the French Revolutionary troops in Paris on Oct. 5, 1795. The government defined that it was a coup.)
(By Charles Monnet (Own work) [Public domain], via Wikimedia Commons)

Napoleon's lofty ambitions matched his rank. He was next tasked with the invasion of England. Knowing that his navy could not defeat the Royal Navy, Napoleon instead proposed to invade Egypt so that British trade routes to India could be cut off. He enjoyed a decisive victory at the Battle of the

▲ Battle of the Pyramids

Pyramids in 1798. 🌐 And then in 1799, seeing an opportunity back in France, Napoleon left Egypt to take up arms against the Directory!

KEY WORDS

- lofty
- ambition
- task
- invasion
- defeat
- the Royal Navy
- propose
- invade
- trade route
- cut off (cut-cut-cut)
- decisive
- opportunity
- take up arms against

Napoleon joined forces for the takeover with Emmanuel Sieyès, one of the new directors, and the coup was successful.  The Directory was replaced with a three-member consulate, and Napoleon became first consul. It was during this time that he made his mark as more than a military strategist. Napoleon would excel as a strong political leader, too.

▲ a portrait of the first consul Napoleon
(Jean Auguste Dominique Ingres
[Public domain or Public domain],
via Wikimedia Commons)

POP QUIZ

Who did Napoleon join forces with in order to stage a coup against the Directory?

ⓐ the King of England
ⓑ Emmanuel Sieyès, a director

KEY WORDS

- takeover
- director
- coup

- be replaced with
- consulate
- consul

- military strategist
- excel

He understood the needs of the people. Napoleon knew the people were tired of civil wars and the chaos in their country. As first consul, he was determined to restore stability to post-Revolution France.

He also embraced many of the ideals of the French Revolution, including liberty and equality. With those traits in mind, he proposed the new and much improved Constitution of the Republic. It provided for freedom of religion and an end to hereditary privilege where men would pass down their possessions and titles to their children. It had been a common practice in Europe's feudal system. Under the new Constitution, there would be equality for *all* men!

POP QUIZ

What did Napoleon wish to achieve as first consul?
ⓐ He wanted to conquer the known world.
ⓑ He wanted to restore stability in France.

KEY WORDS

- need
- be tired of
- civil war (*cf.* civil)
- chaos
- restore
- stability
- post-

- embrace
- ideal
- liberty
- equality
- improved
- constitution
- hereditary

- privilege
- pass down
- possession
- common practice
  (*cf.* practice)
- feudal system

Now, Napoleon began a different sort of campaign, bringing many reforms to France. The terrible squalor in Paris was transformed into a beautiful city, with enchanting parks and boulevards. He founded a better banking system that is still used today. But perhaps his most enduring and impressive legacy is the Napoleonic Code.

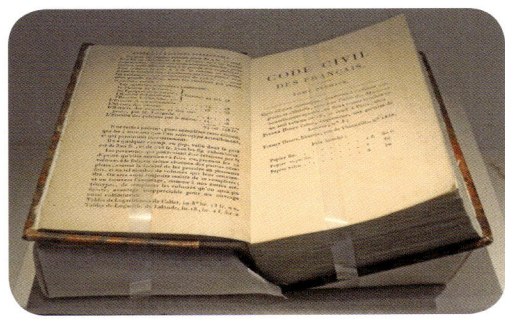

▲ Napoleonic Code

(DerHexer, Wikimedia Commons, CC-by-sa 4.0 [CC BY-SA 4.0 (http://creativecommons.org/licenses/by-sa/4.0) or CC BY-SA 3.0 (http://creativecommons.org/licenses/by-sa/3.0)], via Wikimedia Commons)

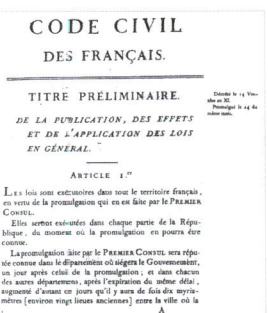

▲ the first page of the original edition of the Napoleonic Code

(By Imprimerie nationale (Scanned image on Gallica) [Public domain], via Wikimedia Commons)

KEY WORDS

- a sort of
- campaign
- terrible
- squalor

- transform
- enchanting
- boulevard
- found

- banking system
- enduring
- legacy
- code

Did Napoleon have a grand vision for his code? It's hard to say, because at the time, he simply wanted to clean up the mess that was France's legal system. There weren't really laws in the country as there were customs, and these were different from town to town. Favors and special privileges had been granted to feudal lords and kings. While these types of special privileges in other areas had been taken away, the legal system had not changed. So Napoleon and his commission worked hard to simplify the judicial system. They established a set of laws for the entire country. Prior laws had been based on a Roman code, written in Latin. Now, the laws were written in French, so that the people could understand them.

The heart of the Napoleonic Code was equality. There would be no more favoritism, and this ideal spread around the globe because Napoleon conquered so many other nations. The Napoleonic Code followed him to Italy, the Netherlands, and Belgium, all the way to Canada and Saudi Arabia. It's easy to see the democratic influence of the French civil code in these countries.

As Napoleon worked to bring equality at home, he managed to build one of the largest armies ever seen as he conquered most of Europe. His efforts were richly rewarded. Napoleon became a consul for life in 1802.

POP QUIZ

How were Napoleon's successful military efforts rewarded?

ⓐ He became a consul for life in 1802.
ⓑ He became Emperor of the World.

KEY WORDS

- have a grand vision
- clean up
- mess
- legal
- favor
- feudal lord
- take away
- commission

- simplify
- judicial system
- establish
- a set of
- prior
- be based on
- favoritism
- spread (spread-spread-spread)

- conquer
- all the way
- democratic
- civil code
- richly
- reward
- for life

But his success only served to attract his enemies. These men did not approve of Napoleon's new order and they decided to assassinate him. Their plans were thwarted, but Napoleon made a decision of his own in 1804. He would crown himself Emperor of France so that other adversaries in Europe would think twice about assassinating a world leader!

▲ Coronation of Napoleon
(Jacques-Louis David [Public domain], via Wikimedia Commons)

KEY WORDS

- serve
- attract
- approve

- new order (*cf.* order)
- assassinate
- thwart

- make a decision
- adversary
- think twice (think-thought-thought)

It seems odd that a man who valued the ideal of equality, who embraced the beliefs of the French Revolution, should choose to rule over all men as emperor. But Napoleon had always been an ambitious man, and besides, the people fully supported him. When his smaller army defeated two of the most powerful countries in the world—Russia and Austria—in 1805, there would be no doubts about the emperor. Napoleon had proved himself as the most brilliant military leader in Europe.

▲ Napoleon who receives the surrender of the Austrian army after the Battle of Ulm
(René Théodore Berthon [Public domain], via Wikimedia Commons)

KEY WORDS

- odd
- value

- rule over
- besides

- prove
- brilliant

But with all his success, Napoleon still had much he wished to achieve. Remember, he was not a man to give up easily. And so when his beloved wife, Josephine, was unable to give him an heir, he divorced her in 1810. He married Marie Louise and shortly afterwards, he had a son, also called Napoleon.

On the military front, Napoleon made the ill-fated decision to invade Russia. He took over 600,000 men into Russia in June, and though he ultimately would take Moscow, it was a long campaign. The bitterly cold winter defeated Napoleon's army. When he returned to France, he had barely 30,000 men. The allied forces of the Austrian and Prussian armies, old enemies of Napoleon, took advantage of the emperor's losses and advanced on Paris. Napoleon abdicated, giving up his throne to Louis XVIII. The once invincible emperor was exiled to the island of Elba in March of 1814. But he would not remain there long.

KEY WORDS

- with all
- achieve
- heir
- be unable to + *Verb*
- divorce
- shortly afterward(s)
- front

- ill-fated
- bitterly
- barely
- allied
- Prussian
- take advantage of
- loss

- advance
- abdicate
- invincible
- exile
- Elba

Napoleon bided his time on Elba, gathering information from loyal supporters. There was unrest in France and the once emperor believed he could take back his country. In March of 1815, he planned a daring escape from the island. It had only taken a year, but Napoleon was back. He entered Paris, greeted by cheers, and the king, Louis XVIII, was forced to flee.

▲ (Charles de Steuben [Public domain], via Wikimedia Commons)

KEY WORDS

- bide one's time
- unrest

- take back
- daring

- be forced to + *Verb*
- flee (flee-fled-fled)

It was, however, a short-lived success for the man who did not believe in the word "impossible." Though he had gathered an impressive army to his side, other European armies rallied against him. Napoleon would fight again, this time at the Battle of Waterloo. 🌐

▲ the image of the Battle of Waterloo
(The Duke of Wellington is in the middle.)
(Jan Willem Pieneman [Public domain, Public domain or CC0],
via Wikimedia Commons)

Napoleon faced his old enemy, Wellington, at this muddy field in Belgium. Both men were the same age, daring military strategists who knew that Europe lay in the balance.

KEY WORDS

- short-lived
- rally
- muddy
- in the balance
- win the day
- overcome (overcome-overcame-overcome)
- battlefield
- in defeat

- attempt
- regain
- abdominal pain
- plague
- former
- stomach cancer
- indomitable

Both armies fought throughout the long hours, and though it looked as if Napoleon would win the day, Wellington's men were at last joined by the Prussian army. It was too much for Napoleon's men to overcome. The French leader would leave the battlefield in defeat, exiled this time to the island of Saint Helena.

For perhaps the first time in his life, Napoleon did not attempt an escape, did not plan an attack to regain his position. It may have been the abdominal pains that plagued him for the last years of his life. Most historians believe that the former emperor died in 1821 of stomach cancer. Napoleon's indomitable spirit would not rise again, but the great military leader's legacy lives on in the democratic ideals seen around the world!

▲ the image of Napoleon who died in bed
(By PHGCOM [Public domain], via Wikimedia Commons)

Comprehension Quiz

A Mark T for true or F for false.

➊ Napoleon ranked 47th out of 58 in his graduating class. T F

➋ Napoleon was put in charge of France's Army of Italy. T F

➌ The new government in France was known as the Directory. T F

➍ Napoleon's forces were outnumbered and beaten severely in 1795. T F

B Circle the right word(s) for each underlined part.

➊ Napoleon wanted to improve France's (legal / economic) system.

➋ There weren't really (laws / customs) applicable throughout France.

➌ Changes needed to be made after the (French Revolution / Battle of the Pyramids).

➍ The new laws were written in (Latin / French), making it easier for people.

C Choose the best answer to each question.

❶ As first consul, which ideals of the French Revolution did Napoleon embrace?

a) liberty and justice

b) religious freedom and the feudal system

c) liberty and equality

d) freedom of speech and religion

❷ Why was Napoleon able to return to France after his first exile?

a) The King of France was not interested in ruling the country.

b) There was unrest in France and many people supported Napoleon.

c) He served his term of imprisonment at Elba.

d) The island of Elba was only a short distance from France.

❸ What is Napoleon's greatest legacy?

a) his famous book on military strategy

b) his democratic ideals from the Napoleonic Code

c) the land holdings of France, won from his battles

d) his descendants throughout the world

Chapter Three

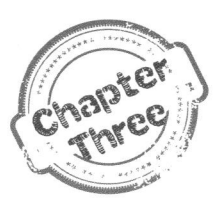

Mahatma Gandhi, Protestor for Change

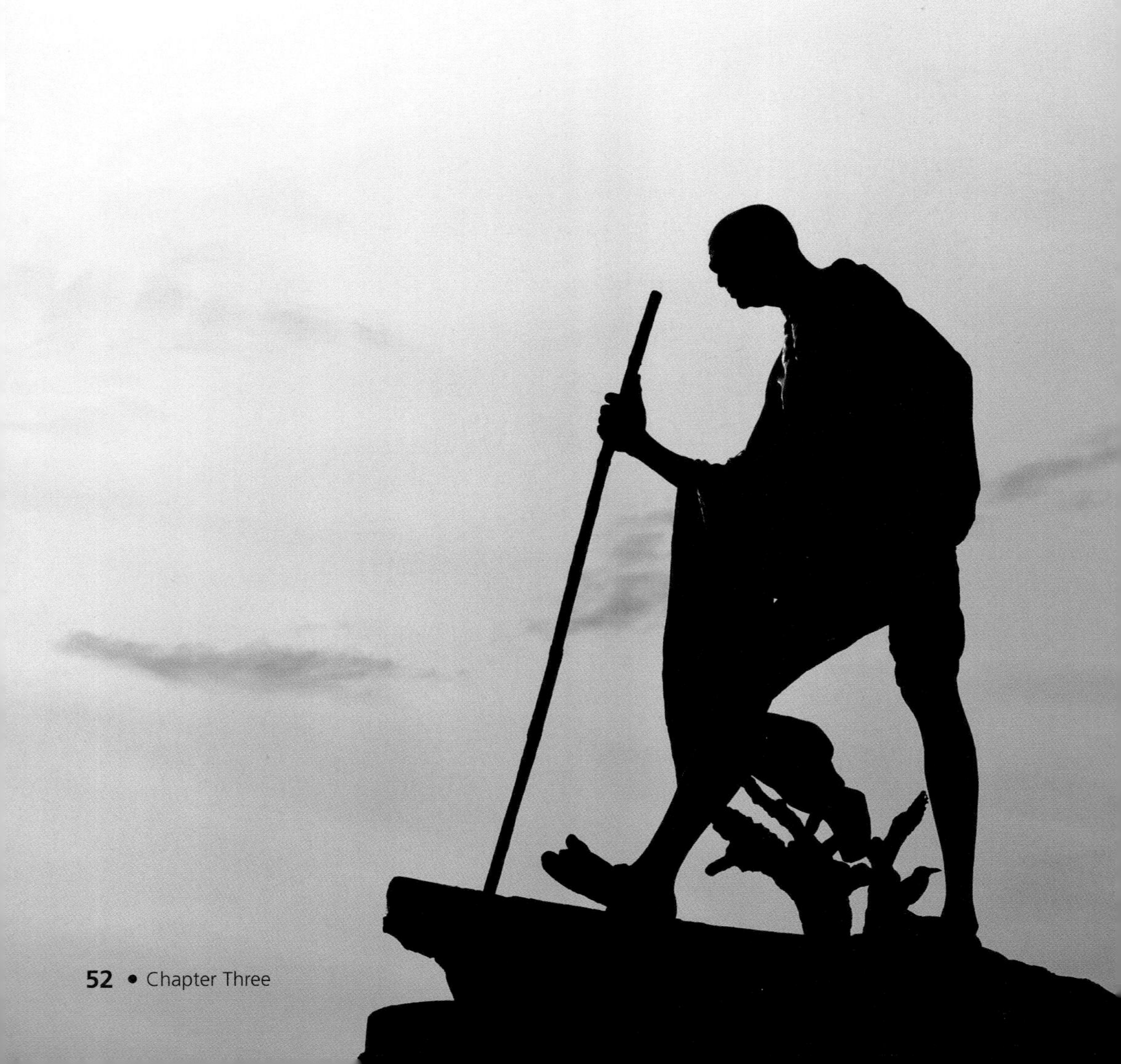

It is said that leaders are often born, not made. But Gandhi did not start out a leader. Truly, he was full of surprises from the very beginning!

The man known as a champion for the poor was born in 1869 into a well-to-do family. He was comfortably raised in the merchant class. His father held a prestigious position in the government and Gandhi was able to attend good schools where he studied English. He was 13 when he married, and even more surprising, he was a rebellious teenager, defying the Hindu beliefs of his devout mother.

▲ young Gandhi at the age of 7
(See page for author [Public domain or Public domain], via Wikimedia Commons)

POP QUIZ

Which of the following is NOT true about Mahatma Gandhi?

ⓐ Gandhi's family was well-to-do.
ⓑ His mother was not very religious.

KEY WORDS

- start out
- truly
- be full of
- surprise
- from the very beginning

- champion
- well-to-do
- comfortably
- merchant
- prestigious

- be able to + *Verb*
- rebellious
- defy
- Hindu
- devout

How did Gandhi change his life and go on to become a larger-than-life leader for change? Several events had a transforming impact on Gandhi, but perhaps most surprising of all is that Gandhi's mission to help Indians took root in *South Africa*!

▲ Gandhi in the Republic of South Africa
(See page for author [Public domain or Public domain], via Wikimedia Commons)

Gandhi studied to be a barrister in London and then returned to India, but in Bombay, he was not a very successful lawyer. He jumped at the opportunity to go to South Africa in 1893, but he was not prepared for the prejudice that met him there.

POP QUIZ

Where did Gandhi practice law when he wasn't successful in India?

ⓐ Great Britain
ⓑ South Africa

KEY WORDS

- go on to + *Verb*
- larger-than-life
- have an impact on
- transforming

- mission
- take root
- barrister
- Bombay

- jump at
- prejudice

Although he dressed in a western style suit, Gandhi also wore a turban. When a magistrate asked him to remove his headdress, Gandhi refused and left the courtroom. And later, even though he was well dressed and had a first class ticket, he was thrown off a train because of his darker skin color.  Forced to spend a bitterly cold night in the station, Gandhi's views were forever changed. He made up his mind to stay in South Africa, and he would fight the injustices he'd witnessed.

KEY WORDS

- turban
- magistrate
- remove

- headdress
- courtroom
- **throw off** (throw–threw–thrown)

- make up one's mind
- injustice
- witness

The young lawyer wanted to put an end to the discriminatory practices against Indian immigrants. Just a few months after the train incident, Gandhi set up the Natal Indian Congress. 🌐 Meanwhile, the seeds of war were spreading in South Africa. With the Boer War in 1899, Gandhi saw an opportunity for the Indians to gain legitimacy. If they would serve in the war, he believed, then surely they would gain their citizenship rights. He organized the Indian Ambulance Corps, with 300 free Indians and 800 indentured, or contracted laborers. This was one of the few medical units set up to help wounded black South Africans, and Gandhi served as a stretcher-bearer.

KEY WORDS

- put an end to
- discriminatory
- immigrant
- incident
- set up
- Natal
- congress

- meanwhile
- seed
- Boer War
- gain
- legitimacy
- citizenship
- right

- ambulance corps
- indenture
- contracted
- laborer
- unit
- wounded
- stretcher-bearer

▲ founders of the Natal Indian Congress(Gandhi is in the top row, fourth from left.)
(See page for author [Public domain or Public domain], via Wikimedia Commons)

▲ stretcher-bearers of the Indian Ambulance Corps during the Boer War
(Gandhi is in the middle row, fifth from left.)
(See page for author [Public domain], via Wikimedia Commons)

But when the war ended, the Indian situation had not improved. In fact, Indians were treated even worse. In 1906, the Transvaal government required all Indians to register.  Gandhi's use of non-violent protest began when he refused to carry an identification card. Indians followed his example, employing peaceful resistance in defying the law. It was not long before they began to pay the price for this passive resistance. Indians were flogged, shot, and imprisoned. Gandhi was arrested, too, and it was in jail, in 1908, that he read Henry David Thoreau's *Civil Disobedience*. Thoreau's words inspired Gandhi even more in his fight for civil justice through non-violent protest.

▲ Henry David Thoreau

KEY WORDS

- treat
- Transvaal
- require
- register
- non-violent protest
- identification card

- employ
- resistance
- it is not long before
- pay the price for
- passive resistance
- flog

- imprison
- arrest
- jail
- disobedience
- inspire
- justice

▲ Indian miners who protest under Gandhi's leadership
(See page for author [Public domain or Public domain],
via Wikimedia Commons)

Next, Gandhi called for a strike to protest against a tax inflicted upon working class Indians, primarily the miners and the farm laborers. In 1913, he led over 2,000 people from Natal to the Transvaal, and though he was arrested and served nine months in prison, Gandhi's efforts were rewarded. The British government dropped the tax and Gandhi was released. Perhaps more importantly, Gandhi's methods of civil disobedience and passive resistance made a mark not just in South Africa but England and India, too. It was time for Gandhi to go home.

KEY WORDS

- call for
- strike
- protest against
- tax
- inflict upon
- primarily
- miner
- release
- method
- it is time to + *Verb*

Gandhi returned to India after more than twenty years away, and he was not happy with the poverty in his homeland. By 1920, he was convinced that Indian independence was the only way to save his country and improve the lives of its people. He began

▲ (See page for author
[Public domain or Public domain],
via Wikimedia Commons)

his campaign for improvement with changes in the Indian National Congress (INC), a major political party. 🌐 But first, Gandhi made a personal change. He began to wear the Indian dhoti, a garment worn by Hindu males that is tied at the waist. Gandhi called the traditional white robe that replaced his suit his "mourning robe." It was his statement of solidarity, or unity, with the poor in India. He never wore anything else.

the flag of the Indian National Congress ▶
(By Own work (Image drawn by me, Nichalp using Inkscape.)
[Public domain], via Wikimedia Commons)

Gandhi worked tirelessly to change the INC. Before, it had been a political party for the elite in India, those who were wealthy and of a high caste, or social class. 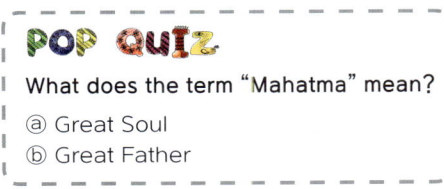 Gandhi brought the INC to *all* the people. No matter the religious faith or class, they would all embrace the idea of the non-violent, non-cooperative protest. And more than anything else, Gandhi wanted India's independence from Britain.

It was during this time that Gandhi would be called by a new name: "Mahatma," a title that means "Great Soul." Others have earned the same title, but none so famous as Mahatma Gandhi!

POP QUIZ

What does the term "Mahatma" mean?

ⓐ Great Soul
ⓑ Great Father

KEY WORDS

- convinced
- independence
- improvement
- party
- dhoti
- garment
- robe
- statement
- solidarity
- unity
- tirelessly
- caste
- non-cooperative
- soul

Unfortunately, it was Gandhi's widespread fame and success that earned him another arrest. Because his resistance movement flourished, the British government put Gandhi in jail for two years. When he was released, Indians still labored under British rule. And so Gandhi protested again.

The British Salt Laws prohibited Indians from selling or collecting salt, and worse, they had to pay an exorbitant tax for British salt. Gandhi led thousands of poor Indians on his Salt March where they boiled up salt from the water. This act was illegal, but the British were unable to control the vast numbers of protesters as well as their various acts of civil disobedience. The British gave in, and Gandhi traveled to London to represent the Indian National Congress at official talks.

▲ Gandhi and Indians on the Salt March
(By Yann (Scanned by Yann (talk).) [Public domain or Public domain], via Wikimedia Commons)

In the end, he failed to gain what he had strived so long for: Indian independence. Gandhi returned to India and vowed to quit politics. But then came World War II. Winston Churchill called for India to support the British in the war, but Gandhi did not think Indians should fight for Britain when they were still under British rule. Thus his next protest called for Britain to "Quit India" for good. 🌐

Churchill refused to back down, and Gandhi and his wife were imprisoned. This time, the protests turned violent, erupting throughout the country! In 1944, he was finally released, but sadly, his wife died months before, while still in prison.

POP QUIZ

What famous British person caused Gandhi to begin the "Quit India" campaign?

ⓐ King George VI
ⓑ Winston Churchill

KEY WORDS

- flourish
- labor
- prohibit from
- exorbitant
- boil up
- illegal (↔ legal)

- vast
- give in
- represent
- talks
- strive
- vow

- quit
- thus
- for good
- back down
- erupt

Gandhi finally achieved independence for India, but it was not

the independence he'd envisioned. Two countries were created from one. The nations of India and Pakistan were divided along religious lines, and tragically this led to chaos, violence, and mass killings! 🌐 War broke out between the two nations. Gandhi left for Calcutta, hoping that through his fasting, he could bring about a new peace. But on his way to a prayer meeting, he was shot three times in the chest.

KEY WORDS

- envision
- divide
- line
- tragically
- mass killing (*cf.* mass)
- break out (break-broke-broken)
- Calcutta
- fasting
- bring about (bring-brought-brought)
- prayer meeting
- nominate
- discussion
- likely
- proponent
- weigh against
- nomination
- short list
- according to
- committee
- suitable
- candidate
- embody
- quote

Perhaps the biggest surprise of all in the life of Mahatma Gandhi was that he never won the Nobel Peace Prize. He was nominated in 1937, '38, '39, '47, and finally, in 1948. There has been much discussion about why Gandhi never received the award. All these years later, it seems most likely that though Gandhi was a strong proponent of non-violence, his protests sometimes led to violence. Sadly, this fact may have weighed against him in the first four nominations. But in 1948, it's clear that Gandhi *would* have won at last. First, because there were only three names on the short list, including, of course, Gandhi.

And secondly, because according to a statement released by the committee, the Nobel Prize was not awarded that year as there was "no suitable *living* candidate." Gandhi had been assassinated on January 30th, 1948. He didn't need to receive any awards. He lived long enough to bring about the changes that would forever change India. He was a leader who truly embodied the quote he's most famous for: You must be the change you wish to see in the world!

▲ (See page for author [Public domain, CC BY-SA 2.0 (http://creativecommons.org/ licenses/by-sa/2.0) or Public domain], via Wikimedia Commons)

Comprehension Quiz

A Put the sentences in order.

❶ Gandhi set up the Indian Ambulance Corps.

❷ Gandhi was kicked off a train because of his skin color.

❸ Gandhi encouraged immigrants to serve in the Boer War.

❹ Gandhi set up the Natal Indian Congress.

_____ → _____ → _____ → _____

B Mark T for true or F for false.

❶ After the Boer War, the Indian immigrants' situation greatly improved. T F

❷ The Transvaal government required all Indians to register. T F

❸ Gandhi carried an identification card in his wallet. T F

❹ Indians would pay a high price for peaceful resistance. T F

❺ The INC had been a party for the elite in India. T F

C Choose the best answer to each question.

➊ Which of the following incidents of prejudice affected Gandhi?

a) A magistrate asked him to remove his turban while in court.

b) He was called names by other lawyers in the courts.

c) He was asked to leave a plane because of his skin color.

d) He was not allowed to ride on public transportation.

➋ How did Gandhi feel about his homeland when he returned in 1920?

a) He was impressed with the level of trade success he saw.

b) He could relax because the country was on track.

c) He thought only Indian independence could save his country.

d) He was relieved that poverty had lessened a great deal.

➌ What happened when Gandhi was imprisoned from 1942~1944?

a) Protests turned violent.

b) Gandhi's wife refused to go to jail with him.

c) The British backed down and granted India independence.

d) Gandhi refused to eat and nearly died.

Nelson Mandela, Imprisoned Freedom Fighter

Another great leader came out of South Africa. He left the freedom of his small village only to end up spending years imprisoned so that others could be free. His name was Rolihlahla, though the world knows him better as Nelson.

Nelson Mandela was born in 1918 in South Africa, the son of the principal counselor to the acting king of the Thembu people. He was sent to a Christian school and there, as was the custom, he was given the Christian name of Nelson. When he was only nine, though, his father died, and Nelson was adopted by a high-ranking member of the Thembus who had plans for the youngster. He wanted Nelson to be a great leader. And the more Nelson learned about the inequalities in his country, the more he was determined to be a leader who would bring great changes to his people. 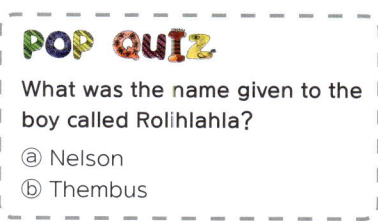 Even as a young man, Nelson Mandela would demonstrate the spirit of protest that marked his long life.

POP QUIZ

What was the name given to the boy called Rolihlahla?

ⓐ Nelson
ⓑ Thembus

KEY WORDS

- freedom fighter
- principal
- counselor
- acting
- Thembu (*cf*. Thembus)
- Christian
- as is
- adopt
- high-ranking member
- youngster
- inequality
- demonstrate

After he finished at Healdtown, a Methodist college, he attended University of Fort Hare, which was the only black institution for higher learning at that time in South Africa. But he was expelled for protesting over university policies. After being kicked out, he returned home in disgrace, where his guardian decided to arrange a marriage for him. But Nelson Mandela wanted to choose his own wife, and so he fled to Johannesburg. Still, he had more on his mind than finding a wife. He studied law through a correspondence course. He met many people who later became key figures in the fight against discrimination. And he joined the African National Congress (ANC). There, he managed the newly formed Youth League. And then, in 1948, the National Party came into power.

KEY WORDS

- Methodist
- institution
- expel
- policy
- kick out

- in disgrace
- guardian
- arrange a marriage
- correspondence course
- key figure

- discrimination
- African National Congress
- Youth League
- National Party
- come into power

Nelson Mandela was thirty years old when the National Party introduced the policy of apartheid in South Africa.  It's not a very big word, but it had a huge effect on black South Africans. The system of apartheid promoted segregation, the enforced

▲ a sign banning black people
(By Dewet [Public domain], via Wikimedia Commons)

separation of people by race. It also permitted discrimination based on skin color. So if you were a black South African, your rights were severely limited.

POP QUIZ

What policy permitted segregation and discrimination in South Africa?

ⓐ apartheid
ⓑ democracy

KEY WORDS

- introduce
- apartheid
- segregation

- enforced
- separation
- race

- permit
- severely

It wasn't long before Mandela and the African National Congress took action in the form of mass civil disobedience. In the campaign for the Defiance of Unjust Laws, Mandela and others traveled across the country. They encouraged protests and attempted to overwhelm the justice system. Nelson Mandela became well known during this time, so it was not surprising when he was arrested on charges of high treason. For five years, the trial continued, and often, Mandela would sleep in jail at night and be allowed to work at his law firm during the day. Eventually, he and the others were acquitted and Mandela was finally free. But Sharpeville was coming.

Sharpeville is just a small township in Transvaal, but in 1960, it was the scene of a massacre that would shock the entire world. Sixty-nine anti-apartheid demonstrators were killed as they protested outside the Sharpeville police station. As chaos and riots swept the country, the government banned the ANC. The time for peaceful protest was over, thought Mandela and his friends. That was the beginning of the development of the military faction of the ANC called "Spear of the Nation."

▲ the graves of 69 people who were killed during the Sharpeville Massacre
(By Andrew Hall (Own work) [CC BY-SA 4.0 (http://creativecommons.org/licenses/by-sa/4.0)], via Wikimedia Commons)

KEY WORDS

- take action
- in the form of
- Defiance of Unjust Laws
- overwhelm
- justice system
- on charges of

- high treason
- trial
- law firm
- be acquitted
- township
- massacre

- demonstrator
- riot
- sweep (sweep-swept-swept)
- faction
- Spear of the Nation

▲ thatched room where Mandela hid
(By Colinvlr (Own work) [Public domain],
via Wikimedia Commons)

It was also the beginning of Mandela going underground. He kept a low profile and stayed in hiding. But at the same time, Spear of the Nation tried to bring the government, in Mandela's words, "to its senses." They blew up railroad lines as well as government buildings. Though they had no policy to take lives, there were accidental deaths. Years later, Mandela would explain the reason behind Spear of the Nation: "It was only when all else had failed, when all channels of peaceful protest had been barred to us, that the decision was made to embark on violent forms of political struggle."

KEY WORDS

- go underground
- keep a low profile
- senses
- blow up (blow-blew-blown)
- take life
- accidental

- behind
- bar
- embark on
- capture
- sentence
- be behind bars

- senior
- suburb
- be implicated
- sabotage
- conspiracy

Mandela was captured in 1962 and imprisoned for leaving the country illegally. At that time, he was sentenced to serve five years. While he was behind bars, though, many of the senior members of the ANC were captured in Rivonia, a suburb of Johannesburg. Mandela was implicated along with the other men, and at the Rivonia Trial, he and the others were sentenced for treason, sabotage, and violent conspiracy. Nelson Mandela would spend the next 27 years imprisoned on Robben Island.

▲ Robben Island Prison where Nelson Mandela was held captive

◄ the inside of Mandela's prison cell
(By Witstinkhout (Own work) [CC BY-SA 3.0 (http://creativecommons.org/licenses/by-sa/3.0)], via Wikimedia Commons)

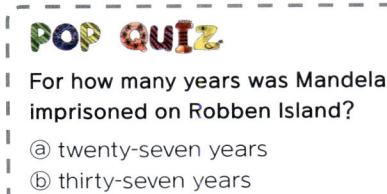

POP QUIZ

For how many years was Mandela imprisoned on Robben Island?

ⓐ twenty-seven years
ⓑ thirty-seven years

He lived in a tiny cell, alone, often stuck in solitary confinement, with no bathroom and no proper bed. He worked in the quarry, too, breaking rocks from sunrise till sundown. The government wanted to break Mandela, to humiliate him so that his followers would scatter. But Mandela continued to protest from the inside of his jail cell. Then, the international community began to gather support for him on the outside.

In 1964, for example, South Africa was banned from the Olympics and economic sanctions were upheld, too. In the 70's, Mandela smuggled out many political statements as well as his autobiography, *Long Walk to Freedom*. Though it was not published for the rest of the world until 1995, many people in South Africa would read his words. And yet, these same people did not know what Nelson Mandela, the man known for anti-apartheid in South Africa, looked like. It was against the law to print photos of him!

KEY WORDS

- cell
- stick in (stick-stuck-stuck)
- solitary confinement
- quarry
- sunrise
- sundown
- humiliate
- follower
- scatter
- international community

- economic sanction
- uphold (uphold-upheld-upheld)
- smuggle
- autobiography
- be published
- prisoner
- racist
- regime
- repeal

In 1980, the *Free Nelson Mandela* campaign began to bring pressure to release South Africa's most famous political prisoner. There were big events, like the music concert for his 70th birthday, when internationally known musicians gathered in support of Mandela. And inside the country there was growing violence against the racist regime. Still, another ten years passed. But on February 11th, in 1990, Nelson Mandela was finally released from prison.  The apartheid laws were repealed by then President FW de Klerk.

Not surprisingly, the end to apartheid was not easy. Conflict and tension ruled the day, but Mandela, with calm resolve, worked tirelessly for reconciliation in South Africa. In 1993, Nelson Mandela and FW de Klerk were awarded the Nobel Peace Prize

▲ Mandela casting his vote in the 1994 election (By Paul Weinberg [CC BY-SA 3.0 (http://creativecommons.org/licenses/by-sa/3.0) or GFDL (http://www.gnu.org/copyleft/fdl.html)], via Wikimedia Commons)

for their efforts in healing the country. And in 1994, when South Africa held its first multi-racial parliamentary elections, Nelson Mandela became the first black President.

Nelson Mandela achieved much as president. He introduced social and economic programs that would improve the lives of black South Africans. A new constitution was enacted that prohibited discrimination against minorities, including white people. He worked towards a goal of a united South Africa. He discouraged blacks from retaliating against old wrongs, and instead, encouraged peaceful unity among all.

KEY WORDS

- conflict
- tension
- resolve
- reconciliation

- multi-racial
- parliamentary election
- enact
- minority

- discourage
- retaliate

Even after Nelson Mandela's presidency ended in 1999, and he retired from politics in 2004, he continued to lead his people. Mandela worked for social justice and peace. He established the Nelson Mandela Foundation and The Elders, organizations devoted to ending human suffering not just in South Africa but around the world.

Nelson Mandela died in 2013 at the age of 95, a man who refused to let a jail cell imprison his dreams of freedom for a nation!

KEY WORDS

- presidency
- retire

- foundation
- elders

Comprehension Quiz

A Mark T for true or F for false.

❶ Mandela studied law through an online university. T F

❷ Mandela managed the newly formed Youth League. T F

❸ Mandela spent 27 years imprisoned at Robben Island. T F

❹ The government wanted to humiliate Mandela. T F

❺ Mandela gave up protesting while he was imprisoned. T F

B Circle the right word(s) for each underlined part.

❶ When Mandela went underground, he went into (<u>hiding</u> / <u>tunnels</u>).

❷ Spear of the Nation blew up (<u>prisons</u> / <u>railroad lines</u>).

❸ Mandela wanted to bring the government to its (<u>knees</u> / <u>senses</u>).

❹ In 1962, Mandela was (<u>arrested</u> / <u>elected</u>) for a second time.

❺ After apartheid was abolished, Mandela did not want blacks to (<u>retaliate</u> / <u>argue</u>), or fight back against old wrongs.

C Choose the best answer to each question.

❶ What organization introduced apartheid into South Africa?

a) the National Party

b) the Democratic Party

c) the African National Congress

d) the Apartheid Agency

❷ What happened when the African National Congress was banned?

a) Mandela and his friends decided to leave South Africa.

b) Mandela and his friends thought the time for peaceful protest was over.

c) Spear of the Nation captured the President of South Africa.

d) Thankfully, apartheid ended and South Africa was at peace.

❸ What was the campaign called that brought pressure to release Mandela?

a) *Music for Mandela*

b) *Free Nelson Mandela*

c) *Let Mandela Go*

d) *Say No to Apartheid and Yes to Mandela*

Mother Teresa, Saint of Calcutta

Mother Teresa may have been small, but that never kept her from doing big things. Perhaps one of her most famous quotes was even inspired by her short stature. "Not all of us can do great things," she often said. "But we can do small things with great love."

Mother Teresa is often pictured in her blue and white sari, the simple dress-like uniform of the Missionaries of Charity. But she had been a nun long before she organized that famous convent. Her road from the schoolgirl named Anjezë Gonxhe Bojaxhiu to Saint Teresa of Calcutta was long and full of twists and turns that would take her all over the world!

▲ (By Manfredo Ferrari (Own work) [CC BY-SA 4.0 (http://creativecommons.org/licenses/by-sa/4.0)], via Wikimedia Commons)

KEY WORDS

- Mother
- saint
- stature

- sari
- simple
- Missionaries of Charity

- convent
- twists and turns
  (*cf.* twist)

Her journey began when she left her home in Skopje, in the Republic of Macedonia, to join the Sisters of Loreto in Ireland to become a missionary. But first, she had to learn English so that she could teach in India. She studied hard and when she was just nineteen, she traveled to Darjeeling, near the Himalayan Mountains, and began to teach at St. Teresa's school. It was here that she would choose the name that today has such worldwide recognition.

Young women studying in a convent take a series of vows before they become nuns. When young Anjezë made her first religious promise, she wanted the name of Saint Therese of Lisieux, also known as the Little Flower of Jesus. But she could not take the name Therese since another nun already had that name. So she chose the Spanish spelling, Teresa, instead. When she took her final vows in 1937, as was the tradition, she took the title "Mother" and became known from then on as Mother Teresa.

KEY WORDS

- journey
- Republic of Macedonia
- Sisters of Loreto (*cf.* sister)
- missionary
- recognition

- take a vow
- a series of
- Lisieux
- minister to
- Bengali

- Hindi
- famine
- despair
- calling

Mother Teresa next taught at St. Mary's High School for Girls, a school that ministered to some of the poorest in Calcutta. Through education, she hoped to ease the suffering of these Bengali girls. Mother Teresa even learned to speak Bengali and Hindi to better communicate with her young charges. In 1944, she became the principal of the school, and though she was distressed at the poverty, famine, violence and despair she witnessed in the city, it seemed as if Mother Teresa's life of service was complete. But then she experienced what she described as "a calling within a calling."

It was 1946, and Mother Teresa was on a train, on her way to a retreat, when she heard Christ speak to her. He told her that she should leave the school and go to work among some of the city's poorest people, in the slums of Calcutta. She was nearly forty years old, but she did not question her calling, even though it took nearly two years for her to convince the convent to let her go. And even when she was allowed to leave, Mother Teresa did not have a clear idea of what she needed to do.

She traded in her habit for a white and blue sari and decided that for the next six months, she would study basic medical training. Then she entered the slums, her only desire was to ease the suffering of the "poorest of the poor" in Calcutta.

It was not an easy task, and many times, Mother Teresa longed to return to the comfort of the old convent. But she refused to give up, even when she was forced to beg for food and supplies herself. She opened a school in the slums and established a home for the dying and poor. Finally, in 1950, she received permission from the Vatican for an order that she called the Missionaries of Charity. It was just a small group, made up of just a few women, mostly former students and teachers from St. Mary's, her former high school. But from this small beginning grew something bigger than Mother Teresa could have ever imagined!

▲ (By flowcomm (Flickr: Missionaries of Charity Mother House) [CC BY 2.0 (http://creativecommons.org/licenses/by/2.0)], via Wikimedia Commons)

KEY WORDS

- retreat
- Christ
- slum
- convince
- trade in A for B

- basic medical training
- desire
- many times
- long
- comfort

- beg for
- supplies
- permission
- be made up of

She and her sisters would minister to thousands upon thousands of people all over the world. In her own words, they cared for "the hungry, the naked, the homeless, the crippled, the blind, the lepers, all those people who feel unwanted, unloved, uncared for throughout society, people that have become a burden to the society and are shunned by everyone."  This mission became orphanages, hospices for those with AIDS, help for refugees, a colony for lepers, and mobile clinics, too. Her charitable work gained attention, and soon, donations poured in so that Mother Teresa could provide homes and help far beyond Calcutta.

As her mission grew, more and more women joined her. Her sisters traveled to Asia, the Americas, Europe, and Africa to help the poor. And wherever they went, they ministered in the faith of those they served. Whether Hindu or Muslim, atheist or Catholic, it made no difference to the Missionaries of Charity. Soon, the sisters were joined by the Missionaries of Charity Brothers and scores of lay volunteers. She was awarded the Jewel of India, the highest honor an Indian civilian can receive. In 1979, Mother Teresa was awarded the Nobel Peace Prize for her work "in bringing help to suffering humanity."

KEY WORDS

- thousands upon thousands
- care for
- naked
- crippled
- leper
- unwanted
- uncared for
- burden
- shun
- orphanage
- hospice

- AIDS
- refugee
- colony
- mobile clinic
- charitable
- gain attention
- donation
- atheist
- make no difference
- scores of
- lay

Despite years of poor health, Mother Teresa continued to lead her sisters and travel globally to serve the poor and dying. But on September 5, 1997, the tiny nun's big heart finally gave out. And yet, that was not the end of Mother Teresa's story. There would be another twist or two in her long journey.

▲ Mother Teresa Memorial House in Skopje

After her death, Mother Teresa's journal writings became public, and in her writings, she often expressed her doubts about her faith. But instead of people losing faith, they were inspired! Mother Teresa's doubts only demonstrated her strong bond with the simple people she came to serve, a bond that would eventually lead to her sainthood!

POP QUIZ

How did Mother Teresa's journal writings affect the world?

ⓐ Her doubts inspired all those who had doubts as well.
ⓑ Her doubts caused many people to stop supporting her.

KEY WORDS

▪ give out
▪ become public
▪ sainthood

In death, as in her life, Mother Teresa administered aid to the sick and suffering. In 2002, the Vatican, the governing head of the Roman Catholic Church, recognized the first miracle attributed to Mother Teresa in 1998. A woman in India had been cured of a tumor after praying for Mother Teresa's help. Thirteen years later, Pope Francis recognized the second Mother Teresa miracle when a Brazilian man with a viral brain infection was cured in 2008 after his family prayed to her.

On September 4, 2016, tens of thousands of people gathered in

▲ canonization
(Pinturicchio [Public domain or Public domain], via Wikimedia Commons)

Rome to attend the canonization of the woman often called "the saint of the gutters" because of her work with the poor. 🌐 Today, she is known as Saint Teresa of Calcutta, a saint who did great things with great love!

KEY WORDS

- **as in** (*cf.* in death as in life)
- administer
- governing
- attribute to
- tumor
- pope
- Brazilian
- viral
- infection
- tens of thousands
- canonization
- gutter
- compassion
- ingenuity

Have you found all the qualities of a great leader among these pages? Compassion, courage, ingenuity, and persistence are a few of them, aren't they? Perhaps you could name even more traits in Queen Victoria and Napoleon, Gandhi and Nelson Mandela, and even Mother Teresa. But ore thing is certain. These men and women did not start out to change the world. They saw a great need and acted, not understanding what a difference they would make. You, too, can develop the characteristics of great leadership, and who can know what a difference *you* might make in the world!

Comprehension Quiz

A Mark T for true or F for false.

❶ Mother Teresa was known to be a tall woman.　　T　F

❷ Mother Teresa believed everyone could do small things with great love.　　T　F

❸ As a schoolgirl, Mother Teresa wore a blue and white uniform.　　T　F

❹ Mother Teresa spent her whole life in her hometown.　　T　F

❺ Mother Teresa's mission became orphanages and mobile clinics.　　T　F

B Circle the right word for each underlined part.

❶ It was very (easy / difficult) for Mother Teresa to help the poor.

❷ Mother Teresa herself had to (beg / steal) in order to survive.

❸ Mother Teresa finally opened a school in the (slums / city).

❹ Mother Teresa received permission from the (Vatican / government) for an order.

C Choose the best answer to each question.

❶ Why is Mother Teresa given the title "Mother"?

   a) It's traditional for nuns to take the title after their final vows.

   b) All nuns who are teachers are called "Mother."

   c) She was the oldest nun and other girls looked up to her.

   d) She'd had a child before she entered the convent.

❷ What did Mother Teresa do before entering the slums of Calcutta?

   a) She gave away all her books and teaching materials.

   b) She traded in her habit for a red and white sari.

   c) She begged for money and food for the poor.

   d) She studied basic medical training.

❸ What awards were given to Mother Teresa?

   a) the Jewel of Macedonia and the Nobel Peace Prize

   b) the Prize for Peace and the Gem of India

   c) the Jewel of India and the Nobel Peace Prize

   d) the Nobel Peace Prize and the International Prize for Humanity

Let's Review the Story

Fill in the blanks to review the story.

Title: Great _____ of the World

Queen Victoria: She holds the record for being the second longest reigning m_____ in Britain. She and her husband brought many reforms to the people, but after Prince A_____ death, Victoria went into m_____ for 25 years. Still, she served her country well and her reign became known as the G_____ Age of Empire, bringing the country peace and prosperity.

Napoleon Bonaparte: He was both a m_____ and political leader who changed not only F_____ but also the world. He conquered many countries and built an empire before his final defeat at the Battle of W_____. Napoleon died in exile, but the democratic ideals of his _____ Code live on today.

Mahatma Gandhi: When he was forced to leave a train in S_____ A_____, he set out to change the system. He called for protest s_____ and encouraged the practice of p_____ r_____. When he returned home, he worked for Indian i_____, and though jailed and eventually assassinated, Gandhi succeeded in bringing much needed changes to I_____.

Nelson Mandela: He had a spirit for f_____! When the policy of a_____ became law in his country, he protested so much that he was imprisoned for 27 years on _____ Island. At last released, he became the first _____ President of South Africa, bringing peace, equality, and freedom for all the people.

Mother Teresa: The tiny nun believed that everyone could do "_____ things with great _____." She left home to become a m_____, but Christ called her to live in the s_____, helping the poor. She started a new order, the M_____ of Charity, and today, the work of Saint Teresa of Calcutta continues all over the world.

Let's Think & Talk

Think about the following questions and answer them freely.

❶ Organize the achievements of the leaders in the book.

❷ Explain what similarities and differences the leaders in the book have. Tell your friends what thing(s) two or more leaders have in common and what is unique to each leader.

❸ Among the leaders in the book, which one do you admire the most and why?

❹ Do you know any other great leader? Search for information about his or her life and achievements, organize your notes and tell your friends about that person.

Let's Review the Story

Title: Great ┃Leaders┃ of the World

Queen Victoria: She holds the record for being the second longest reigning ┃monarch┃ in Britain. She and her husband brought many reforms to the people, but after Prince ┃Albert's┃ death, Victoria went into ┃mourning┃ for 25 years. Still, she served her country well and her reign became known as the ┃Golden┃ Age of Empire, bringing the country peace and prosperity.

Napoleon Bonaparte: He was both a ┃military┃ and political leader who changed not only ┃France┃ but also the world. He conquered many countries and built an empire before his final defeat at the Battle of ┃Waterloo┃. Napoleon died in exile, but the democratic ideals of his ┃Napoleonic┃ Code live on today.

Mahatma Gandhi: When he was forced to leave a train in ┃South┃ ┃Africa┃, he set out to change the system. He called for protest ┃strikes┃ and encouraged the practice of ┃passive┃ ┃resistance┃. When he returned home, he worked for Indian ┃independence┃, and though jailed and eventually assassinated, Gandhi succeeded in bringing much needed changes to ┃India┃.

Nelson Mandela: He had a spirit for ┃freedom┃! When the policy of a┃partheid┃ became law in his country, he protested so much that he was imprisoned for 27 years on ┃Robben┃ Island. At last released, he became the first ┃black┃ President of South Africa, bringing peace, equality, and freedom for all the people.

Mother Teresa: The tiny nun believed that everyone could do " ┃small┃ things with great ┃love┃." She left home to become a ┃missionary┃, but Christ called her to live in the ┃slums┃, helping the poor. She started a new order, the ┃Missionaries┃ of Charity, and today, the work of Saint Teresa of Calcutta continues all over the world.

Smart Readers: **Wise** & **Wide**

After-reading Test

- Great Leaders of the World
- Level 6
- 27 Questions

  (Vocabulary 7 / Reading Comprehension 16 /

  Sentence Structure & Grammar 4)

1. Which of the following pair has the wrong past tense form of the verb?
   ① set – set
   ② put – put
   ③ flee – flee
   ④ spread – spread

2. Which of the following is NOT a word represents a person?
   ① pioneer
   ② trailblazer
   ③ squalor
   ④ vendor

3. Which of the following is similar to the word "transform"?
   ① build
   ② change
   ③ travel
   ④ carry

※ Choose the right word for each blank. (4~5)

4.
   > Victoria was responsible _____ many reforms that eased the suffering of the poor.

   ① at   ② of
   ③ for   ④ with

5.

> The Directory was replaced _____ a three-member consulate,
> and Napoleon became first consul.

① up   ② of
③ into   ④ with

※ Choose the common word for the two blanks. (6~7)

6.

> • Her beloved husband, Albert, died _____ typhoid fever in
>   December of 1861.
> • Napoleon knew the people were tired _____ civil wars and the
>   chaos in their country.

① of   ② for
③ with   ④ into

7.

> • In 1863, in fact, the railways and the London Underground were
>   built, thanks _____ her support.
> • She was unable _____ give him an heir.

① on   ② of
③ to   ④ against

8. What happened in 1840 that changed how Queen Victoria ruled?
    ① Victoria's mother died.
    ② Lord Melbourne was no longer prime minister.
    ③ Victoria married Prince Albert.
    ④ Victoria married an Italian prince.

9. What was the Great Exhibition sometimes called?
   ① Albert and Victoria's Exhibition
   ② the Crystal Palace Exhibition
   ③ the Mighty Museum Exhibition
   ④ the Crystal Museum Exhibition

10. What was said when the monarchy doubled in size during Victoria's reign?
   ① The sun rises and sets in England.
   ② The sun never sets on the British Empire.
   ③ The sun and moon reign in Britain.
   ④ The sun always sets in the east of England.

11. What was Napoleon working toward in Corsica, in 1789?
   ① He was attending school in France.
   ② He was hoping to free the island of French rule.
   ③ He was in his homeland, applying for a government position.
   ④ He was in Paris, studying military strategy.

12. Which of the following was NOT a reform that Napoleon brought to France?
   ① an improved Constitution of the Republic
   ② an end to the feudal system
   ③ a new banking system
   ④ an improved water and sewage system

13. Why did the Napoleonic Code spread throughout the world?
    ① People asked Napoleon to share his ideals.
    ② Napoleon brought his code to the countries he conquered.
    ③ The code was easy to understand since it was written in English.
    ④ Everyone who heard about the code wanted it, too.

14. Why was it odd that Napoleon would crown himself Emperor of France?
    ① He believed in the ideals of the Revolution, including equality.
    ② He had never liked the idea of royalty.
    ③ He was not ambitious at all and did not want to rule.
    ④ He was born on Corsica and was not a native-born Frenchman.

15. What was the result of Gandhi's call for a strike in 1913?
    ① The government forced Gandhi out of South Africa.
    ② Though he was imprisoned, a tax was dropped.
    ③ It became obvious that passive resistance didn't work.
    ④ Taxes were raised even higher and Indians were flogged.

16. Why was the Nobel Peace Prize NOT awarded in 1948?
    ① There was "no suitable living candidate."
    ② There were too many candidates on the short list.
    ③ There was no money to give to the winner.
    ④ The committee could not award the prize during a war.

17. Which quote is Gandhi most famous for?
   ① "You must be the man you wish to be in the world."
   ② "You must quit India or die."
   ③ "You must be the change that you wish to see in the world."
   ④ "You must always try to do your best every day."

18. What was Mandela arrested for during the Rivonia Trial?
   ① treason, violent conspiracy, and arson
   ② sabotage, arson, and murder
   ③ treason, sabotage, and violent conspiracy
   ④ murder, treason, and lying

19. What is the title of Mandela's autobiography?
   ① *Long Walk of Protest*
   ② *27 Years in Prison*
   ③ *Long Walk to Freedom*
   ④ *Protesting for Freedom*

20. Who was the first black President of South Africa?
   ① FW de Klerk
   ② Winnie Mandela
   ③ Nelson Mandela
   ④ William de Klerk

21. Why did Mother Teresa go to the Republic of Ireland?
    ① She joined the Sisters of Loreto to become a nurse.
    ② She joined a convent there to learn about computers.
    ③ She was ready to see the world and learn English.
    ④ She joined a convent to become a missionary.

22. Who were some of those that Mother Teresa and her nuns served?
    ① the criminals, the rich, and the doctors
    ② people who could pay for assistance
    ③ the crippled, the blind, the lepers
    ④ men who lived in the suburbs of India

23. What did the Vatican recognize so that Mother Teresa could be canonized?
    ① evidence of miracles
    ② proof of magic
    ③ evidence of wealth
    ④ kindness

※ Choose the wrong part of each sentence. (24~25)

24.
Even if he was well dressed and had a first class ticket, he was
    ①   ②   ③

thrown off a train.
    ④

25.

> And <u>so</u> he returned <u>to</u> the island, <u>spending</u> his time <u>study</u> strategy.
>   ①   ②   ③   ④

26. What is the common word for the blanks?

> They cared for _____ hungry, _____ naked, _____
> homeless, _____ crippled, and _____ blind.

① a   ② the
③ people   ④ many

27. What is the correct sentence?
① But for February 11th, in 1990, Nelson Mandela was finally released from prison.
② But on February 11th, in 1990, Nelson Mandela was finally released from prison.
③ But from February 11th, in 1990, Nelson Mandela finally released from prison.
④ But at February 11th, in 1990, Nelson Mandela finally released from prison.

Memo

Memo

Cathy C. Hall

Cathy C. Hall graduated with a broadcasting degree, working in the radio industry as a news reporter and commercial copywriter before going back to school to earn English certification. She spent a decade in education, teaching preschoolers, middle schoolers, and high schoolers. Now, she's a full-time freelance writer, with stories, essays, and poems in publications for both children and adults. Her byline appears in books like *Uncle John's Facts To Annoy Your Teacher*, *Chicken Soup for the Soul's Think Positive for Kids*, *Cup of Comfort for Dog Lovers*, and many more.

 Smart Readers Wise & Wide 6-9

Great Leaders of the World

Written by Cathy C. Hall
Illustrated by Yeonjo Kim

First Published in August 2017

Editorial Manager: Juyon Choi
Editors: Kyunghee Jang, Jiyeong Park
Designer: Eunhee Lee
Cover Designer: Eunhee Lee

Published and distributed by

 Happy House

Darakwon Bldg., 64-1 Jandari-ro, Mapo-gu, Seoul, Korea 04031
Tel: 82-2-736-2031(ext. 250)   Fax: 82-2-732-2037
Homepage: www.ihappyhouse.co.kr
Publisher: Kyudo Chung

ISBN: 978-89-6653-547-7 18740 / 978-89-6653-156-1 18740(set)

[Components]
• 1 Audio CD (Recording Studio: Aram)
• Answer Keys & Korean Translation: Free download at www.ihappyhouse.co.kr

Image Credit: shutterstock.com / Wikimedia Commons